FARM ANIMALS

Written by
Eliza Nodes

Genius Kid

sales@northstareditions.com I 888-417-0195

Library of Congress Control Number:
The Library of Congress Control Number is available on the Library of Congress website.

ISBN
979-8-89471-056-3 (library bound)
979-8-89471-076-1 (paperback)
979-8-89471-114-0 (epub)
979-8-89471-096-9 (hosted ebook)

Printed in the United States of America
Mankato, MN
012026

Written by:
Eliza Nodes

Edited by:
Sadie Hallworth

Designed by:
Ker Ker Lee

Photo Credits – Images courtesy of Shutterstock.com, unless otherwise stated.

Cover – Eric Isselee, Gabriel Dominella, Anzki, Elkin Restrepo, Eric Isselee, Clara Bastian, Bas Kuijstermans, BearFotos, photomaster, MisterStock, DnD-Production.com. 2–3 – Dmytro Leschenko, 06photo. 4–5 – DnD-Production.com, BigTunaOnline. 6–7 – Eric Isselee, Mr. SUTTIPON YAKHAM. 8–9 – kirill_makarov, Clara Bastian. 10–11 – ilknurvelizarova, Herman Vlad, photomaster, kittirat roekburi, tristan tan. 12–13 – Marti Bug Catcher, Michael Siluk, photomaster, Studio Romantic. 14–15 – MaraZe, Hong Vo, JeniFoto, Artem Avetisyan, cemsimsek, Richard P Long, Elnur. 16–17 – Svietlieishyi Andrii, M Stocker, Le Do. 18–19 – Ground Picture, Ewa Studio. 20–21 – klublu, paha1205, LeapingLizard, JACKREZNOR. 22–23 – StockEU, Clara Bastian, Khosro, Clara Bastian, Ihor Hvozdetskyi, Passakorn Umpornmaha.

CONTENTS

Words that look like this can be found in the glossary on page 24.

COWS

What do you think of when you hear the word *cow*?

Do you imagine a black-and-white spotted coat? Do you imagine a farmer collecting milk?

Cows are mammals. They are warm-blooded, have a backbone, and make milk to feed their young.

Cows are part of a group called the Bovidae or bovine family. Cows are female bovines. Bulls are male bovines.

Cows are herbivores. They eat only plants.

Most cows are domesticated, which means they are kept by people. Most domestic cows live on farms.

BODY OF A COW

Cows have hooves. Each hoof is split into two parts. These hooves are called cloven hooves.

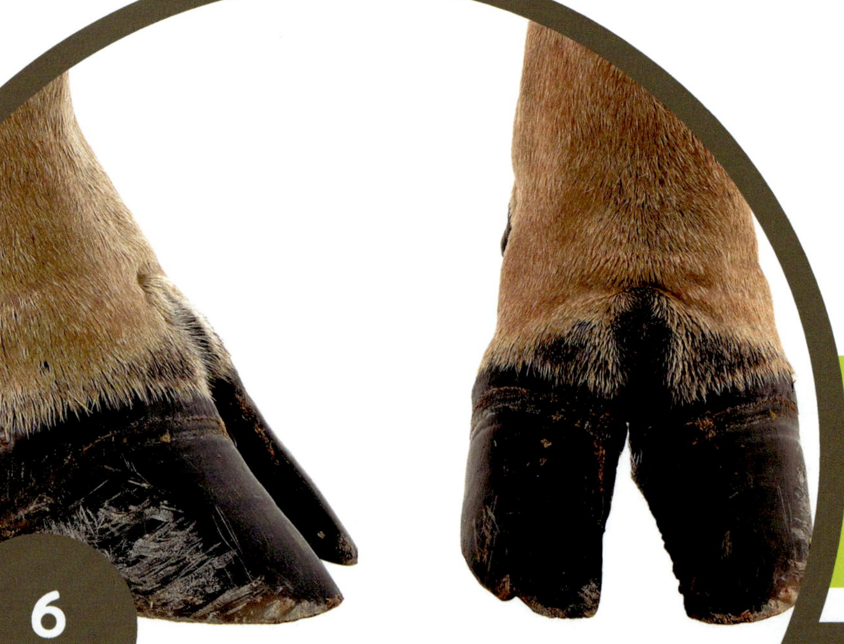

DID YOU KNOW?
The two parts of a cow hoof are called claws.

Cows' stomachs are split into four parts called compartments. These compartments help cows break down the grass they eat.

Cows regurgitate their food. They rechew it many times. This helps them get as many nutrients as possible from their food.

Like all mammals, cows make milk to feed their young. Once cows have had young, milk comes out of their udders.

FACE OF A COW

Cows that live on farms often have plastic tags in their ears. This helps farmers know which cow is which.

Cows have a good sense of smell. They can smell things nearly 6 miles (10 km) away.

Cows' eyes are on the sides of their heads. They can spot dangers from almost every direction.

Thick whiskers help cows find their way through tight or small spaces.

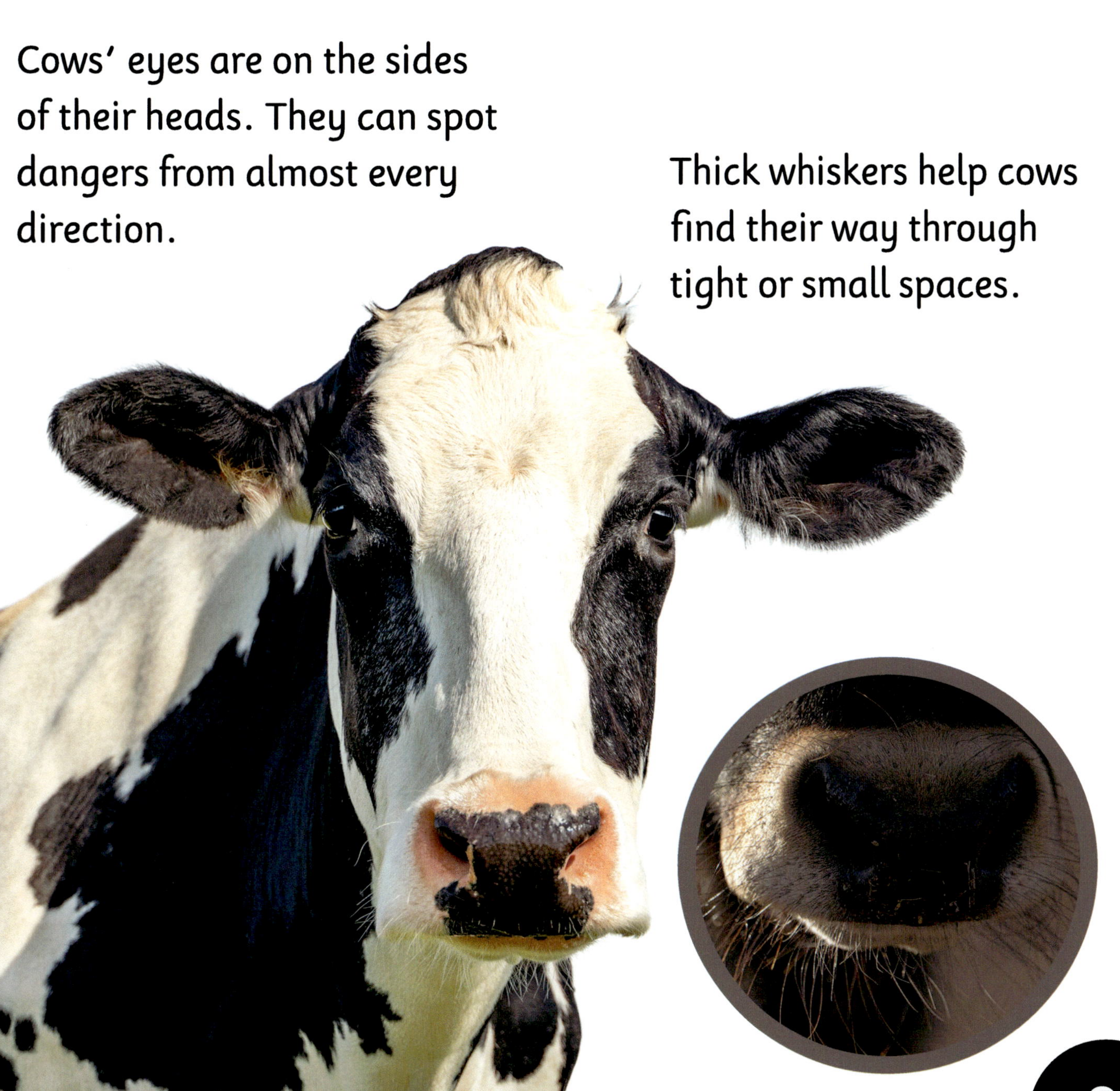

BREEDS OF COWS

There are many kinds of cows. Different types are called breeds. Humans make breeds by controlling which bovines have young together.

Aberdeen Angus cows have black skin and hair. They do not have horns.

Holstein-Friesian cows have black-and-white coats.

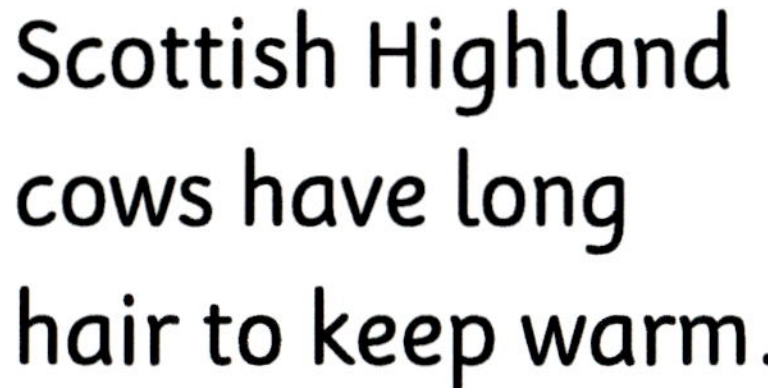

Scottish Highland cows have long hair to keep warm.

Watusi cattle are known for their long horns. The horns can grow more than 8 feet (2.4 m) long.

Brahman cows first came from India. They have a large hump over their shoulders.

LIFE ON THE FARM

On farms, many cows live in buildings called barns.

Some cows live outside when the weather is right. Farmers bring them inside when it is too hot or too cold.

Cows spend around six hours eating every day.

Cow food is made from a mixture of different plants. It includes hay and grains such as corn, soybeans, and wheat.

DID YOU KNOW?

Cows drink enough water to fill a bathtub each day.

HOW PEOPLE USE COWS

Most cows and their milk are made into food.

Cow meat is called beef. Beef is made into food such as burgers and steaks.

Dairy cows make milk. Milk is made into food such as cheese and ice cream.

Cow skin is made into leather. Leather can be used to make many things, including shoes, jackets, belts, and car seats.

Cow poop is used as a fertilizer. Farmers spread it on fields to help plants grow.

FROM CALF TO COW

Baby cows are called calves. Calves drink their mothers' milk when they are first born.

Cows make more milk than their calves can drink. So, farmers collect the extra milk. Cows can make milk for 10 months after having calves.

A heifer is a young female bovine. Heifers become cows when they have their first calf. Farm cows usually have around 10 calves throughout their lives.

Cows can live for around 20 years. Cows raised for meat usually live for up to two years. Dairy cows usually live for around six years.

LOOKING AFTER COWS

Farm cows have vet checkups once or twice a year. Vets make sure the cows don't have any illnesses. When cows are pregnant, vet checkups happen more often.

DID YOU KNOW?
A vet is a doctor for animals.

Calves need to be vaccinated to stop them from catching and spreading illnesses.

Cows are herd animals. They like living in groups. Being with other cows helps them feel safe and happy.

BELIEVE IT OR NOT!

Hundreds of years ago, cows were a sign of wealth. The number of cows someone had showed how rich they were.

In some religions, such as Buddhism and Hinduism, cows are seen as sacred. There are even laws to protect cows in some countries.

Cows have best friends! They can become stressed when separated from their pals.

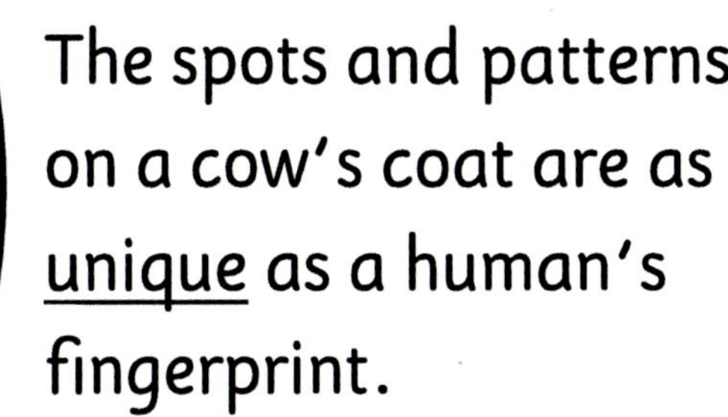

The spots and patterns on a cow's coat are as unique as a human's fingerprint.

ARE YOU A GENIUS KID?

Now you know all about cows. Your friends and family are going to be so impressed! But how much can you remember? It's time for a quiz!

Check back through the book if you are not sure.

1. What is the name of the group cows are a part of?
2. How do cows find their way through small spaces?
3. When do heifers become cows?

Answers:
1. Bovidae
2. They feel with their whiskers.
3. once they have had their first calf

GLOSSARY

breeds groups of animals that are bred to have similar characteristics

family a way of grouping animals with very similar traits

fertilizer a substance added to soil to help plants grow

nutrients natural substances that plants and animals need to grow and stay healthy

regurgitate to bring partly broken-down food up from the stomach to the mouth

sacred worthy of respect and awe

unique one of a kind or very rare

vaccinated injected with a medicine to protect against a disease

INDEX